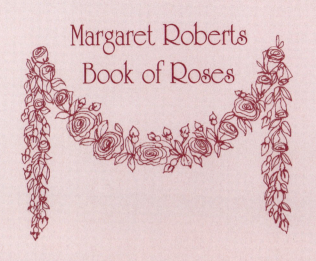

Margaret Roberts Book of Roses

Margaret Roberts Book of Roses

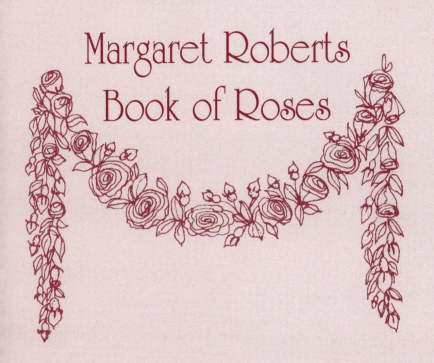

SOUTHERN
BOOK PUBLISHERS

Copyright © 1993 by Margaret Roberts.

All rights reserved. No part of this publication may be
reproduced or transmitted in any form or by any means without
prior written permission from the publisher.

ISBN 1 86812 480 0

First edition, first impression 1993

Published by
Southern Book Publishers (Pty) Ltd
PO Box 3103, Halfway House, 1685

Cover design by Tumbleweed Designs
Illustrations by Margaret Roberts
Set in University Roman 11 on 13.5pt
by Joan Baker
Printed and bound by National Book Printers, Goodwood, Cape

Use only organically grown roses for the recipes in this book.
Never use chemically sprayed or fertilized roses for any
beauty treatments, medicines or food.
Discuss all treatments with your doctor first.
All recipes use fresh rose petals,
fresh rosehips and fresh herbs.

CONTENTS

Introduction	1
Growing roses	3
The rose as a beauty and cosmetic treatment	21
The rose as a medicine	41
The rose in food and cooking	50
The rose in pot-pourri	59
Epilogue	69
Index	72

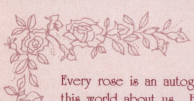

Every rose is an autograph from the hand of God on this world about us. He has inscribed his thoughts in these marvellous hieroglyphics which sense and science have, these many thousand years, been seeking to understand.

Theodore Parker

Roses are God's thoughts of beauty, taking form to gladden mortal gaze; bright gems of earth, in which perchance, we see what Eden was — what Paradise may be!

Anonymous

What a desolate place would be a world without flowers? It would be a face without a smile; a feast without a welcome. Are not flowers the stars of the earth? And are not our stars the flowers of heaven?

Clara L. Balfour

Catmint

INTRODUCTION

No other flower the world over has captured man's imagination, inspired his thoughts and dreams and epitomised his sense of beauty and romance the way the rose has.

The heart flower, as it was once named, is the most loved of all flowers and has always inspired man's artistic sense. Its beauty has been celebrated in legends, poetry, art, decoration, song and dance through the centuries. Whether through the creation of a rose garden, a work of art, food, cosmetics or beauty treatments, the rose has always been a source of wonder and delight.

Many years ago I read somewhere a short verse that has lingered in my memory and I think of it each time I arrange my bowl of roses. It goes something like this:

> *No woman can surely place*
> *A bowl of roses on the shelf*
> *Without the inner upward surge*
> *To be more beautiful herself.*

One can lose oneself in roses, my mother so often said. They soothe, they encourage, they comfort, and as we grow older they stand steadfast as beautiful treasured friends, giving of themselves in all seasons, blooming for us unstintingly and lifting our troubled spirits.

So this little book is a celebration — a celebration of roses, inspired by a wonderful event in my life.

In the heat and drought and tumult of these early nineties, in the hills north of Pretoria, a fragrant, exquisite, full-bodied, old-fashioned rose was born amidst the profusion of roses from all over the world on Ludwig Taschner's rose farm. It stood strong and vigorous, withstanding the searing winds, the pulsating heat and the many desolate, drought-filled months. Water became scarcer and scarcer, the hot winds burnt many a rose's tender petals and still this rose stood tall and upright, buffeted from all sides. Its soft, many-petalled flowers filled the air with rich perfume, and as the flowers opened, so the petals in the tight centre deepened in colour, layer upon layer of shell pink in all its hues, to finally shower themselves in a carpet of beauty at the feet of this sturdy, weather-resistant bush. A plant for this harsh Africa of ours had been born, flowering in spite of every hazard, in prolific abundance and perfect beauty and standing firm.

That this symbol of hope amidst the strife should be called the Margaret Roberts Rose is an honour that will for all time humble and yet inspire me to stand, as it does, in spite of life's blows. For this reason I have been inspired to write about roses, in gratitude and delight, to share the wonder and to inspire you in turn to grow a rose, or two, or a hundred, for that pure, sheer joy in God's most exquisite of all creations.

So, come walk with me through my garden of roses, page by fragrant page, and enjoy with me the glory of the rose...

Growing Roses

There are many books on the subject of growing roses, all written by experts, which I am not. But, having lived for most of my adult life on the slopes of the great Magaliesberg, both the southern and northern sides, I have learnt to fight the relentless elements and have formed through years of sheer hard experience, a sort of survival pattern for my roses and myself!

I have had the added advantage of parents who created beautiful gardens, and my mother, an artist, cultivated roses in my happy childhood years as few others did. I remember well the breathtaking fence of Paul Scarlet in its dark green and massed red spring extravagance, the tall standards of headily fragrant Talisman, the masses of Icebergs and Queen Elizabeths, and the great bowls and garlands and fragrance with which our home was filled. How lovely it was to grow up with roses.

Alongside this beauty was my father's huge compost pit. His Saturday chore was to fill a wheelbarrow with this dark, friable, sweet, earthy mixture and to lovingly spread and dig it in around the roses. He taught me how to make compost and at the age of seven or eight I was pretty competent! I learned to dig big holes for the new roses and to leave them open in the winter sunlight to warm for several days. Then I saw the careful mixing and moistening of good loam and well-matured compost and the cone of soil built up in the hole on which the new rose would perch its roots, to be guided down the sides into the rich depths.

Now, having lived through too many droughts, I add half a bucket of those remarkable water absorbable Terra Sorb crystals (available from nurseries) to each hole. When soaked for an hour in water these crystals swell to a moist, jelly-like mass and, once covered with soil, will maintain a core of moisture on which the roots will feed in times of a water shortage. This has sustained my roses through bleak periods when all else wilts around them.

I compost well twice yearly, usually early in August and again in January, and I am careful to mulch well around each rose. I find the best mulch to be of raked leaves and not grass clippings. Sometimes I mix in some roughly cut veld grass and rosemary clippings and never have a problem with hatching insects in the mulch. When mulching or composting, always make sure the budding union is above the soil.

I water twice weekly — not a sprinkling, but a long, slow filling of the hole around the rose with its high dam around it, the hose only half open so as not to wash out soil and expose the roots. During drought I water deeply only once a week, and check my mulch at the same time.

Natural Fertilisers

As I use no harmful sprays or synthetic fertilisers, I depend totally on insect-repelling plants, natural fertilisers and companion planting.

There are four excellent natural fertilisers which can be dried and

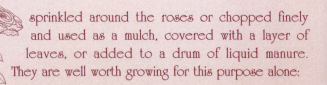

sprinkled around the roses or chopped finely and used as a mulch, covered with a layer of leaves, or added to a drum of liquid manure. They are well worth growing for this purpose alone:

Comfrey (*Symphytum officinale*) Cut three or four times a season. See recipe below.

Sage (*Salvia officinalis*) Well known, incidentally, for sprinkling dried under grapes to give them sweetness, sage is grown in some areas in Israel as a crop for just this purpose.

Lucerne (*alfalfa*) Cut as you would comfrey.

Stinging nettle (*Urtica dioica*) Always use gloves when handling nettles. It is worth growing a clump of bulbinella (*Bulbine frutescens*) in case you are stung. The juice applied frequently will immediately soothe the sting and any rose thorn scratch too.

COMFREY FERTILISER
Mix together 1 bucket of roughly chopped comfrey leaves, half a bucket of sage leaves and sprigs, 3 buckets of kraal manure and half a bucket of wood ash (not coal ash) in a large drum of water (I use an old 44 gallon drum). Let it stand for 2 weeks, giving it a daily stir with a spade. It will rot fast and smell awful!

Water a bucket of this (rotting leaves included) around each rose (never onto the plant itself, but water the outside perimeter of the "dam" around each rose so that it seeps towards the centre). Within a day or two you'll notice a glossiness of leaves, an abundance of new growth and surely an unsurpassing fragrance in each rose! This is the only fertiliser I use. Comfrey is a natural growth stimulant and builds superbly strong branches.

Insect-Repelling Herbs for Roses

Visitors to my herb garden, especially nurserymen, are amazed that my roses are never sprayed! They cannot believe that every one is insect free and conduct a careful search for aphids under the leaves, to find not one. The reason for this is that my roses are surrounded by herbs that are superb insect repellents and make excellent hedges, groundcovers and companion plants.

Camphor basil
Ocimum kilimandscharicum
Indigenous to Africa, this is a particularly useful natural insecticide and makes an attractive flowering bush. It grows to about 1 or 1,5 m in width and height and needs to be pruned. I do so all through the year and it can be trained into interesting shapes and topiaries, or clipped into a fragrant hedge. The oil in the leaves is an excellent insect repellent and leaves and flowering sprays can be added to sprays or mulches throughout the year. I plant camphor basil behind other plants as it protects them from all sorts of infestations. Having a small root system, it does not drain the soil of nutrients.

Catmint
Nepeta mussinii

Another excellent groundcover under roses — no aphid can stand it — is the exquisite, palest mauvy blue and grey catmint. It makes a frothy carpet under the rose bush. I love it best under my pink roses and edging paths, where it spills over softening every stone and hard edge.

When you do need to trim or prune back, you'll find it has rooted in little tufts. These can be dug out and planted elsewhere. I have had much pleasure in creating a pink and white rose garden that is completely covered in catmint. It is a froth of blue and grey all summer long and there is no sign of an aphid, nor, as a matter of interest, a patch of mildew. Catmint can also be added to insect-repelling sprays and to the compost heap.

Cotton lavender
Santolina chamaecyparissus, S. neopolitana

Both varieties of this popular plant make superb hedges and insect repellents and their grey feathery leaves are another perfect foil for roses. S. *chamaecyparissus* is more compact in growth than its close cousin S. *neopolitana*. A spray of cotton lavender, camphor basil and rosemary is particularly useful for treating scale and red spider.

COTTON LAVENDER INSECTICIDE SPRAY
Pour 1,5 buckets of boiling water over 1 bucket of cotton lavender,

camphor basil and rosemary. Mix well and stand covered overnight. Stir and strain the next morning. Add 2 cups of soap powder and 2 cups of bicarbonate of soda. Stir until dissolved. Spray morning and evening onto the roses, skip a day, then repeat. Should it rain, spray again immediately after the rain.

Horsetail
Equisetum ramosissimum
Horsetail is a very worthwhile plant to grow for its remarkable properties as a natural mildew treatment, particularly for roses. *Equisetum ramosissimum*, an indigenous variety, is a rather strange-looking, brittle grass with jointed, leafless stems. It sends up runners all over the place, so do contain it in a back border where it can spread a little.

Horsetail mildew treatment
As a mildew treatment for roses, horsetail is surprisingly quick and effective. In stubborn cases I apply it two or three times a week.
Gather a bucket of horsetail. Dry by spreading on newspaper in the shade. When completely dry, burn. Allow the ash to cool, then carefully gather it. (I burn it in an old galvanised dustbin lid which makes it easy to gather the ash.) Mix with water in a ratio of 1:4. Then splash onto plants by dipping a bunch of leafy twigs (rosemary works beautifully) into it and briskly spattering the plant with it. Be careful not to choose that rare and exquisite thing, a rainy day, for this job! Choose a hot sunny day so that the ash dries on the leaves.

Alternatively, use a comfrey and nettle brew instead of pure water to add to the ash. The brew acts as a foliar feed.

Gather half a bucket of roughly chopped comfrey leaves and nettle sprigs (remember your gloves). Pour over it 1 bucket of boiling water, stand and cool overnight. Strain. Next morning, add to the horsetail ash — 1 bucket of brew to a quarter of a bucket of ash.

Khakibos
Tagetes minuata
Khakibos is an exceptional base for an insect-repelling spray. It will come up as a weed — nurture it, it is invaluable!

Lemon thyme
Thymus citriodorus
This is a very worthwhile groundcover. It is evergreen, compact and pretty and in summer its tiny mauve flowers are much loved by bees and butterflies. There always seems to be much activity around it! This is another herb with a shallow rooting system and there is both a golden variety, T. *citriodorus aureus*, and a silver variety, T. *citriodorus alba*. All three are simply lovely planted under roses and when walked upon emit a strong lemony fragrance.

This herb is well worth experimenting with as I have recently found the roses under which it grows never have any mildew. Black spot has never been a problem for me with interplantings and perhaps in the future these herbs with their rich oils may even be the answer to that age-old problem.

Lemon thyme can be picked and pruned often and used in sprays and insect-repelling liquid manures. Like sage, it has certain nourishing qualities for plants and I am convinced that we need to experiment further with this deeply fragrant groundcover.

Marigold
Tagetes spp.
Marigolds are exceptionally important for insect-repelling sprays. It is definitely worth growing a row or two, for these can be constantly cut back and used for rose sprays. Sprigs can be dug into the soil to keep free from nematodes and insects. Its incredibly pungent oils are an exceptional insect repellent and it is also a superb companion plant for all roses and vegetables.

Myrtle
Myrtus communis
Myrtle is more of a small tree than a shrub and can be clipped into interesting shapes or a hedge. Its oil-rich leaves are excellent in insect-repelling sprays. I find myrtle a perfect background for roses and use clippings as mulches and in sprays not only for roses, but for vegetables too. Crushed seeds are effective in ant holes – just pushed down – and also make an excellent mole deterrent.

I specially grow myrtle for its exquisite sprays of small glossy leaves, white flowers and waxy little buds and berries. I use these in my rose posies for an outer fragrant frill. It's the perfect foil for the multicoloured brightness of the rose blooms.

Myrtle mole deterrent

Mix equal quantities of crushed myrtle seeds, fresh garlic, coriander and mustard seeds. Pound into a paste, moistened with ammonia, tie into small gauze bundles, moisten again with ammonia and push these down mole holes. Cover the opening with a piece of slate or a flat stone to concentrate the fumes.

Pennyroyal
Mentha pulegium

Pennyroyal is a most useful groundcover to use between paving stones in the rose garden or under the roses. Its mauve flowers grow in whorls up the stem and need to be cut back once they start to fade. Like all the *Mentha* species, this mint will constantly seek new ground, often dying back where it was first planted.

It is remarkable in its insect-repelling properties. When tread upon it releases a strong peppermint smell which immediately sends insects scurrying. It also makes an excellent spray.

Pennyroyal insect-repelling spray

Boil pennyroyal in enough water to cover. Leave to stand overnight and use it either as a spray or pour it over a badly infested rose bush. Aphids, ants and mealie bugs will literally wash off dead.

Pyrethrum
Chrysanthemum cinerariifolium

This long-used insecticide is happily coming back into favour once again, and is now more readily available than it once was. I find this pretty and undemanding plant simply charming amongst my roses. It forms a low feathery greyish-green clump, out of which grow white daisies on 20-30 cm stems. It is non-encroaching and easily managed. Just cut off the spent flowers and save them for sprays. Dried flowers can be ground and powdered for an excellent contact insecticide to sprinkle around ant holes or made into the following superb spray for red spider, aphids, scale and mealie bugs.

Pyrethrum spray
Steep 120 g pyrethrum powder (made by grinding the dried flowers) in 150 ml methylated spirits. Stand overnight. Next morning add to 50 litres of water. Spray plants at dusk, when the bees and ladybirds have flown home.

Remember the solution will decompose quickly in heat and sunlight and if you spray at dusk, the plants will be safe for bees and butterflies by morning. Pyrethrum is non-toxic to mammals and is non-accumulative, so it is safe to use on roses that are to be used in food and in cosmetics, and even on cats and dogs for ticks and fleas.

Rosemary
Rosmarinus officinalis
Rosemary is prolific, bushy and exquisite. I love using McConnel's blue rosemary (*Rosmarinus officinalis* var. McConnel's Blue) as a hedge. It is easy to clip into shape, and remains neat, evergreen and beautiful all year through. In fact, it is one of the few

plants that never has an off period! Use the clippings in compost and in sprays. Its strong oils are disliked by aphids and ants and even rosebeetles.

Creeping rosemary
Rosmarinus protratus
This is a superb groundcover under roses, as its small root system does not encroach on the roses' nutrients. Wherever I have grown it, I have never seen a single aphid. Like its tall cousin, it can be clipped and trimmed and its mass of palest blue flowers are a pure pleasure under roses. Use it in sprays like ordinary rosemary.

Rue
Ruta graveolens
Pungent and powerful, rue grows to about a metre in height and width and benefits from being pruned, so it makes an excellent hedge. Crushed rue leaves can be pushed down ant holes or sprinkled around roses. It has non-invasive roots and forms the base for a superb natural insecticidal spray.

Rue insect repellent
Mix half a bucket of rue leaves with half a bucket of mixed herbs (for example basil, marigold, southernwood, coriander, myrtle, rosemary, winter savory, pennyroyal). Pour over 2 buckets of boiling water and leave to stand overnight. Strain and add 2 cups of soap powder. Spray or splash onto roses to keep aphids away and pour it around the plants to deter ants.

Southernwood
Artemesia abrotanum
This herb is bushy and feathery and makes a good hedge. It has a pungent scent. Crushed leaves or sprigs tucked behind books will keep fishmoths at bay. Boiling water poured over a bucketful of sprigs and left to cool overnight makes a simple and effective multi-purpose spray. Southernwood grows to about 60 cm in height and width, needs full sun and benefits from regular pruning. It tends to become straggly, which is why it is so suitable for a trimmed hedge as clipping makes it dense and neat. I sprinkle the clippings around my rose bushes on top of the mulch and I find this keeps crickets away. (Crickets usually love to nestle under mulches!)

Tansy
Tanacetum vulgare
Tansy has strong antiseptic properties, as well as being one of the ancient insect-repelling plants. It has been used for many thousands of years as a "strewing herb" and was once the base of disinfectants and "sewer treatments". It also works against mildew and crushed leaves strewn around rose bushes help to keep insects away. Once when I was desperate to get rid of rose beetles I hooked tansy leaves onto the rose thorns! Tansy spray is superb against aphids.

Cut the tall flowering heads off once they are fully open to encourage more leaf growth. The heads can reach a metre in height and are, incidentally, beautiful in flower arrangements, bringing their spicy pungent scent indoors to freshen a smoke-filled room. I use tansy mostly as a groundcover. Curly tansy (*Tanacetum vulgare* var. *crispum*) can be used in the same way, although it is not as vigorous and does not have the spreading habit of its close relative.

Wild Ginger
Tetradenia riperia (formerly *Iboza riperia*)
This is one of South Africa's own wonder plants. It was used as a malaria remedy and its pungent spicy ginger oils are well known as insect repellents. It cannot withstand frost, but in spring its froths of palest mauve, pink or white flowers make up for its winter barrenness. The leaves are rich in oils and it grows fairly tall and wide, so you will have a lot of leaves in summer from only one plant. Grow wild ginger as a hedge and save the clippings.

A Karroo gardener I know crushes a leaf and tucks it into the rose as it opens. He never has a problem with beetles!

I chop leaves as a mulch and use them in sprays. The bush needs pruning and the same Karroo farmer presses twigs into the soil right inside his rose bush and lets them root there, before pulling them out and transplanting. He swears that's why his roses are show-perfect!

Wilde als
Artemesia afra
Wilde als is another indigenous herb and is used in exactly the same

way as southernwood and wormwood. It grows up to 1,5 m high and needs to be clipped frequently as it becomes very straggly. It makes a good hedge. At a time when I experimented with aphid infestation and ladybird protection, I used sprays of wilde als laid criss-cross over the rose bush and found that it got rid of the aphids and did not affect the ladybirds. Wilde als makes an excellent spray.

Winter savory
Satureja montana

This is my favourite groundcover. It makes a superb evergreen carpet under trees and in early summer is covered in a mass of tiny white flowers. Its mere presence acts as a consistent natural insect repellent. The aromatic leaves can be added to sprays and spent flowering heads can be clipped off and added to sprays, compost and mulches. The roots are not very vigorous, which means that like pennyroyal, creeping rosemary, catmint and lemon thyme, winter savory is ideal for planting under rose bushes – no insect will cross it.

Wormwood
Artemesia absinthium

This has probably been the most esteemed healing herb through the ages, but I find it equally remarkable as an insect repellent. It grows about 50 cm in width and height and tends to become very untidy if left untended. Clip and prune it frequently – it makes a good hedge – and mix every leaf and sprig into mulches, compost and sprays. A few sprigs in the holes in which you plant your new roses will keep cutworms and their friends away from the roots.

Yarrow
Achillea millefolium

This medicinal plant with its mass of pink and white flowers looks spectacular in midsummer circling the rose garden or edging a path leading to the rose garden. It not only acts as a foliar feed when used as a spray, but is also a superb repellent for insects and helps remove mildew, since, like rosemary and myrtle, it is rich in oils. Cut the flowers off to ground level as soon as they fade. Flowers and leaves can be used in the sprays.

BASIC NATURAL INSECT-REPELLING SPRAY

Vary this basic recipe according to the availability of insect-repelling plants. I find that a mixture of four or five different plants works best, but in different areas with different soils you may find some more effective than others.

For example, I found that on the southern slopes of the Magaliesberg, rue, southernwood and khakibos were very effective. On the hotter northern slopes, where I now live, I need to add camphor basil, santolina and often wilde als or wormwood. At different times of the year your mixture will also change in intensity.

Whatever the reason, it is helpful to keep a notebook with details and dates and thus experiment according to your own particular needs. This recipe is really only a guideline and I'm excited to say several rose growers currently experimenting with it are getting most satisfying results. The next step will be for nurseries to sell a six-pack of insect-repelling herbs with every rose bush!

Gather a bucket of mixed insect-repelling herbs, such as yarrow, pennyroyal, winter savory, camphor basil and khakibos. Pour over this 2 buckets of boiling water and stand covered over night. Strain the next morning and add 2 cups of soap powder (I prefer Sunlight soap powder). The following are optional: 1 cup of paraffin (for intense infestation) and 2 cups of wood ash, if available.

Mix well, strain through muslin again if necessary and spray or splash onto plants, ideally for two days running. If necessary repeat three or four days later for two days running.

Rose Beetles

I can't think of anything that raises my fury so quickly as seeing a beautiful rose desecrated by voracious rose beetles! Picking them off by hand is supposedly the only way to control them but since you can't be there all the time to check, the solution is to place a big yellow plastic bucket - the brightest yellow you can find — in the centre of your rose garden, half fill it with water and add 1 cup of paraffin. The beetles will dive-bomb into this amazing, gigantic yellow "flower" (it seems that all insects love yellow). They'll drown quickly as the paraffin fills their spiracles (air holes) and every evening you'll joyfully empty the bucket with its multitude of dead beetles onto the compost heap, especially those CMR

yellow and black jobs that do so much damage.

I was once told of a very macabre way of ridding the garden of rose beetles. Catch several, cut off their heads with secateurs and string them on long black threads all over the roses and fences. The other beetles will take fright on seeing their decapitated brothers and flee! I can't bring myself to try this, but for what its worth I leave you to decide!

The Rose as a Beauty and Cosmetic Treatment

For its perfume alone the rose is perhaps the best loved of all cosmetic and beauty preparations. Commercially every product with a rose fragrance or claiming to contain rose essence, even if it is synthetically coloured and scented, is an assured steady seller.

But how infinitely more satisfying it is to make your own rose beauty preparations — and how sensible in this economic climate. This chapter will inspire you to make your own lotions and creams, using your own roses.

The first recorded rose perfume, known as "otto of roses", was extracted around 1612 by the Persians. The discovery of this exquisite rose oil is a fascinating tale. The story goes that in 1612 an emperor and his princess got married. In order to impress other royal households and visitors during the festivities, the emperor ordered canals to be dug around the palace gardens. These were filled with water and fresh roses. The emperor took his princess on a boat through these fragrant canals and she noticed, while letting her hand hang in the water, that an oily layer had collected under the petals in the sun. The oil was carefully collected on linen gauze and squeezed into perfume bottles. Its exquisite fragrance was called otto of roses, or rose attar.

About 30 roses are needed to extract one drop of oil and in modern day science roses are distilled for use in aromatherapy, medicines and the perfume industry. Synthetic oils make the previous attar of roses available to all at a far cheaper price, but once you have smelled and touched the real thing, you'll undoubtedly discriminate!

One of the most wonderful beauty aids used for decades is old-fashioned rose water. It is still available at chemists but I make my own since I use it lavishly. I use red or pink scented roses to obtain a pretty colour.

Remember that only unsprayed, untreated roses will do in all the recipes that follow. Never use chemically sprayed rose petals for any beauty preparation. Your own homemade natural insect-repelling sprays are fine, but do rinse the flowers under the tap if you have recently sprayed.

Rose Water

Collect 3 cups of fresh petals. Bruise them gently in a pestle and mortar (use only glass, china or unchipped enamel utensils). Pour 2 cups of distilled water over the petals and heat in a double boiler for 20 minutes. Keep the lid on and allow the water under it to just simmer. Cool, still covered, and strain. Bottle into sterilised screw-top bottles and store in the fridge.

For oily skins 1 teaspoon of tincture of myrrh can be added (buy this from your chemist). Be sure to shake it well to disperse the myrrh. This will add to its astringency, and as a bonus will help to preserve the rose water.

Use your fragrant rose water on a pad of cotton wool to freshen and tone the facial skin and neck. I also use it on my elbows and hands. It tones, softens and freshens one beautifully. Take a small bottle of rose water with you when travelling to refresh you and relieve fatigue.

I keep little cotton wool pads in my handbag for just purpose and my skin never feels dirty or greasy, even after a 12 hour trip.

I also add rose water to my bath — about half a cup — when I'm tired and soak my face cloth in it and rub it over my neck and feet to get rid of fatigue. When you start making your own rose water, you will find many uses for it. Try soaking your nails in it after removing nail polish. Soak for about 10 minutes and then buff your nails until they are pink and shiny.

Patting rose water onto the skin before moisturising will plump up lifeless cells and make your skin glow.

Rose Freshener

I keep a bottle of this in my car for an instant refresher in the mid-summer heat, especially on long journeys. It will not only quickly revive you, but will also give your skin a glow and a softness that is immediately noticeable.

Boil 1 cup of rose petals in 2 cups of water with 10 cloves for 10 minutes. Keep covered all the time, then cool. When completely cool, strain and add equal quantities of Perrier or Schoonspruit water. Mix and store in the fridge. Put some freshener in one of those handy pump spray bottles — nurseries often sell them as plant misters. Use lavishly and frequently — even on your arms and legs and the back of the neck. It is a lifesaver on a sweltering day.

This is also excellent when applied as a skin toner before moisturising.

Rose bath milk
This falls somewhere between an oil and a moisturiser, for it is a perfect skin softener, toner and relaxant. Stress lines will disappear, tense muscles will unwind and you'll emerge peaceful, radiant and silky!

Put a few drops of rose essential oil into 2 cups of powdered milk. Mix in 2 cups of rose petals and 1 cup of oats. Place in a 30 cm square of voile or muslin and tie with a ribbon. Loop the ribbon over the tap and turn on the hot water. The powdered milk will quickly dissolve and the oats and petals will soften. Now add enough cold water to ensure a pleasant temperature. Add 1 cup of rose water to your bath water, lie back and relax. Use the muslin ball of petals as a scrub with soap, if desired, and rub yourself all over. Lie back again and relax. I am never able to resist floating a few fragrant petals in the water too for the visual effect.

Moisturisers

In this dry, hot country of ours moisturising the skin is essential to maintain its softness and youthfulness. One needs to be reminded that the outer layers of the skin are actually dead and moisturising is therefore a necessity.

Rose moisturiser
Crush 1 cup of rose petals lightly in a pestle and mortar. Place in a double boiler with 1 cup of aqueous cream and half a cup of glycerine. Melt, cover and simmer for 30 minutes. Strain through muslin, pour into a screwtop jar and apply liberally to dry skin. I love it on

 my feet and it works wonders when rubbed into rough heels with a pumice stone.

Rich rose moisturiser

This is particularly good for very dry, ageing skin but do a patch test first to ensure that it is suitable to your skin. Use as a hand and nail cream, massaging deeply into the nails and cuticles, and also on elbows, legs and feet. It is excellent as a facial moisturiser, especially when you have been gardening in the winter wind or swimming in the summer heat. Used sparingly on the face, it will soothe and soften immediately.

Lightly crush 1 cup of rose petals in a pestle and mortar. Pour 2 cups of boiling water over the petals, cover and set aside for 30 minutes.

In the top of a double boiler melt 2 tablespoons of anhydrous lanolin or beeswax, 100 ml almond oil and 3 teaspoons wheatgerm oil. Stir constantly with a wooden spoon until well blended. Remove from the heat.

Strain the brew and measure off 30 ml (add the rest to your bath water). Gently whisk it into the oil mixture, a little at a time. Finally add a few drops of rose essential oil for fragrance and pour into clean, screwtop jars.

Rose emollient cream

This is a superb wrinkle cream. I use it as a night treatment on crow's-feet, under the chin and on the neck — a little goes a long way.

Make only a tiny amount at a time to ensure that it is fresh when used.

Mix together 1 dessertspoon of lanolin and half a cup of lightly crushed rose petals, mashing down well with a wooden spoon. Add 1 tablespoon of almond oil and 2 teaspoons of apricot kernel oil. Melt in a double boiler. Simmer for 10 minutes. Strain and add the contents of four vitamin E oil capsules. Stir well and pour into little jars. Seal well.

Rose oil
I use softening rose oil for anything, from cracked nails to cracked heels, and have it constantly on hand. I rub it into dry lips and elbows and add a teaspoonful to my bath, especially in winter. I even use it as a base for rose essential oil, adding a sweetly scented synthetic rose oil. I shake it well and pour a little over cloves, cinnamon sticks and coriander seeds to "fix" the fragrance (see section on pot-pourris, page 59).

Pure rose softening oil
Gather a large bowlful of every scented rose you can lay your hands on. Strip the petals from the calyx, add the stamens and the calyx, and pound together with a little almond oil. Do small quantities at a time and fill a large glass jar with the oily pulp. Leave to stand in the sun for a day.

The next day, warm the mixture in a double boiler and simmer for 30 minutes. Cool for an hour, keeping it covered all the time, then strain and pour into small sterilised bottles.

I find it best to make small quantities and if I am going to keep the oil for a long time – say over winter – I store it in the fridge. The secret is to pound as many roses as you can in as little oil as possible in order to really saturate the oil with rose petals.

Attar of Roses

This is a simple way to make that exquisite rose oil discovered by the Persians. Remember, you would need about over 200 000 roses to make about 1 tablespoon of real oil! But it's great fun to try. This precious oil can be used as a perfume. It can also be mixed with almond or any other carrier oil and used as a glorious massage oil.

Fill a large jar with the petals of any fragrant rose. Cover with pure water (rural borehole water, rain water collected far from city smog and dirt, or filtered city water). Stand for seven days in the sun, keeping it covered and turning the jar so that all sides get the warmth of the summer sun.

By the end of the fourth day you'll notice tiny droplets of oily yellow scum rising to the surface. This is it – attar of roses! Use cotton wool wrapped around a match to mop it up, and squeeze it into a sterilised wide-mouthed jar with a screwtop lid. You must mop up the oily scum as often as it appears. On very hot days I do it four or five times. Keep your jar of attar of roses away from light and closed at all times. I use a brown glass jar and keep it in a cupboard.

Quick Rose Massage Oil

This is a quick way to make a lovely, relaxing massage oil.

Find a large, shallow enamel meat dish or a large, heat-proof glass lasagne dish. Fill with scented rose petals and stamens. Cover with spring water or pure borehole water, place on a heated tray such as you use to keep food hot and cover with the dome. Check frequently to see when the oily scum rises, mop it up with damp cotton wool and squeeze into a jar. After 3 hours add enough almond oil to disperse over the water. Leave to diffuse for 3 hours. Mop that up and then dilute with more almond oil. This is particularly soothing massaged into aching legs and sore, stiff muscles.

Rose oil by the enfleurage method
This is the old-fashioned method of extracting oil from any fleshy fragrant flower like the rose, violet, tuberose, honeysuckle and jasmine.

Put a layer of clean cotton wool or thick lint in a shallow glass dish or enamel pan. Dribble with any good oil until it is well saturated. Spread a thick layer of rose petals over this and then put another layer of oil-soaked cotton wool or lint on top. Cover with a clean piece of glass slightly smaller than the pan, and finally with a layer of plastic to keep it airtight. Place in the sun.

Replace the petals every 24 hours – sometimes I have to do it five or six times to get the fragrance I desire. Squeeze out the petals onto the oil-soaked "blanket" before discarding them. Finally squeeze the oil out of both pieces of cotton wool into a light-proof, airtight container.

Use the oil as a fragrant and exquisite massage oil or

add a drop or two to your bath. To deeply cleanse your face, massage a little rose oil into the skin. Then steam your face by making a towel tent over a bowl of boiling water to which a sprig of myrtle or one or two yarrow leaves have been added. Rinse with tepid water mixed with a dash of rose vinegar.

Rose vinegars for hair and body

Vinegar restores the natural acid balance of skin and hair, and is happily coming back into favour, since it is the easiest of all home cosmetics to make.

Standard rose petal vinegar

This is a water-softening vinegar with endless uses. I use it lavishly in my bath to refresh and revive myself after a long, hot day. It also makes a lovely gift.

Take a bottle of white grape vinegar, pour out a little and fill the bottle with rose petals. I mix red and pink roses to give it a beautiful ruby colour. Some pink and yellow petals will make it go brown, but the end-product is equally effective.

Let the bottle stand in the sun and give it a daily shake. Strain and remove the petals after three days and add fresh ones (always use the same kind of petals for each bottle). Let it stand in the sun once again. Replace the petals once or twice more depending on the strength you wish to attain. Finally, strain the vinegar, remove the petals, pour into a pretty bottle and label.

Apple cider and rose vinegar

This vinegar is made in the same way as the one above, but using apple cider vinegar makes it particularly useful for problem skins since it helps to eliminate oiliness. Splash on the face after washing, or dab onto pimples and acne. The smell disappears immediately.

Rose and maidenhair fern bath vinegar

If you live in the city with hard chemical water or in an area known for its hard water, this is superb for adding to your bath or to the water used to rinse your hair. If you do not have maidenhair fern (*Adiantum capillus-veneris*) you can use indigenous hard fern (*Pellaea calomelanus*), comfrey leaves, garden violet leaves (*Viola odorata*) or scented geranium leaves (*Pelargonium graveolens*). All of these soften the skin and added to the rose petals make a superb vinegar that will soften even the hardest water.

Mix a large bottle of white grape vinegar with an equal quantity of apple cider vinegar. Pack in equal quantities of rose petals and fern, or experiment with any of the other herbs mentioned above. Let it stand in the sun for 10 to 14 days. During that time replace the petals and herbs with fresh ones at least three times. Finally, strain and rebottle, adding a fresh sprig for quick identification.

Rose and rosemary hair vinegar

This is my favourite hair rinse. I use it not only as such, but also add half a cup to my bath at the end of an exhausting day to relax me completely. Leg cramps may be relieved by soaking towels in warm

rose and rosemary vinegar and wrapping these around the legs. Relax for 30 minutes with the towels in place.

Make the vinegar in the same way as described above, but use equal quantities of red or pink rose petals and rosemary. The red and pink petals give the vinegar a beautiful, deep red colour.

Added to the final water in which you rinse your hair, it will stimulate hair growth and rebuild brittle hair. It can also be combed into the hair daily as a scalp massage.

Apple cider vinegar can be substituted for grape vinegar and to encourage hair growth even further, you can add half a cup of bruised fenugreek seeds. Leave to draw.

Spring Rose and Jasmine Vinegar
This is a spring must! Gather jasmine flowers and the first rosebuds and then proceed in the same way as for rose and maidenhair fern vinegar. Jasmine is one of the first spring flowers and has a softening effect on the skin. With the rosebuds you can imagine what a delight this is. It makes an exquisite Christmas present.

Rose Petal Face Packs
When I lecture on natural skin and hair care, I always encourage the students to pamper themselves one day every month. We're all running far too fast and as a result we are too fraught, anxious and exhausted to enjoy the beauty of the day or to pause and smell the roses along the way!

One day every month you should concentrate on your hair, skin and nails. Slowly indulge in face packs, hair and skin treatments using natural preparations. They are so easy to make and leave you feeling marvellous.

I always begin with a face pack to rid the skin of deep grime and soften and smooth away all the care and tension lines. As for all the other recipes, I use only fresh, unsprayed rose petals.

Bracing fruit and rose face pack

Perhaps I should call this remarkably refreshing face pack a skin tonic. It tones and strengthens the muscles under the skin, and also tightens the skin. Use any of the following fruit when in season: strawberries, melons, grapes, ripe pears or paw-paws.

Mince 1 cup of rose petals (I use a chopper). Mash or liquidise about half a cup of fruit and mix into the petals. Wash your face, tie your hair back and lie down on a pillow covered with a towel. Spread this luscious mixture over your face and neck, avoiding the eyes. Close your eyes and consciously relax for 15 minutes while listening to soothing music.

Rinse off with lukewarm water to which a dash of rose and apple cider vinegar has been added. Pat dry, freshen with rose water, moisturise (see page 25) and then give your skin a rest — do not put on make-up for a day.

Rose milk and honey face pack for ageing skin

This is an exquisite treatment for softening and smoothing wrinkles.

Mince 1 cup of rose petals. Warm half a cup of milk and stir into it 1 tablespoon of honey. Add half a cup of oats. Stir until it thickens to a porridge-like consistency, cool until pleasantly warm, then add the rose petals. Wash your face in tepid water, tie your hair back, lie down on a pillow covered with a towel and spread the mixture all over your face and neck and, if there is any left over, on the back of the hands. Rest for 15 to 20 minutes consciously steering your mind from any anxious thoughts. Think of roses and lilies and perfumed gardens!

Rinse off with lukewarm water — add a dash of rose petal vinegar — and a soft sponge. Freshen with rose water, moisturise and do not put on make-up for the rest of the day.

ROSE AND CUCUMBER REFRESHER PACK
This is the perfect treatment for an oily, spotty skin.

Mince 1 cup of rose petals, grate 1 cup of cucumber and mix together. Keep two slices of cucumber whole. Wash your face in tepid water, tie your hair back, lie down on a towel-covered pillow, spread the mixture over your face and neck and place the cucumber slices over your eyes. Relax for 15 to 20 minutes.

Rinse off with lukewarm water to which a dash of rose and apple cider vinegar has been added (see page 31), and moisturise lightly with the simple rose moisturiser (see page 25).

Rose and yoghurt face pack

This is particularly helpful in refining coarse skin and enlarged pores and also benefits blemished skin.

Mix together 1 cup of minced rose petals, half a cup to a cup of plain yoghurt and 1 tablespoon of lemon juice. Tie your hair back and wash your face in tepid water. Lie down on a towel-covered pillow, spread the mixture over your face and neck, avoiding the eye area, and relax for 15 to 20 minutes.

Rinse off with lukewarm water to which a dash of apple cider and rose vinegar has been added. Pat dry. Freshen with rose water (see page 23) and moisturise with the simple rose moisturiser (see page 25).

Almond meal and rose pack

This is my most luxurious treat and I do it twice a year. It cleanses deeply, acting almost as a scrub, while tightening, toning and nourishing the skin, leaving it glowing and supple. I love it!

Grind together 1 cup of rose petals and half a cup of almonds. Mix with a little homemade rose-water (see page 23) to a thick paste. Tie your hair back, lie down on a towel-covered pillow, apply the paste to your clean, dry face. With a little of the paste, scrub the areas where dirt accumulates, such as around the nose and chin and at the base of the ears. Leave to dry while you relax for 20 minutes.

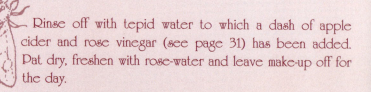
Rinse off with tepid water to which a dash of apple cider and rose vinegar (see page 31) has been added. Pat dry, freshen with rose-water and leave make-up off for the day.

Rejuvenating Egg and Rose Pack

This suits all skin types and is the perfect revitaliser. I use it to lift my spirits after a stress-filled day, usually while reclining in a bath filled with rose petals and a little rose oil.

Beat up a whole egg until frothy. Beat in 1 cup of minced rose petals and 1 tablespoon of honey. Tie your hair back and lie back in the bath — I prop a small rolled towel under my neck. Spread the mixture onto your face, neck and chest, and even the back of your hands if there is any left. Relax for 15 minutes, letting it dry. Rinse off, pat dry, dab on rose water all over and then work in a rich moisturiser like the one on page 26. Lie on your bed and read or simply relax for a while to feel all the benefits of this revitaliser.

Soap Making

There are many recipes for making soap from scratch. Living on a farm, I made my own soaps with lye, sheep or pig fat and olive oil. It was a lengthy, tricky and somewhat dangerous process, since lye burns the skin, and with animals and little children around it is not to be attempted. The ingredients are expensive (unless you slaughter your own animals!) so I use grated bought soaps — the experts do it far better than I ever have. Should you want to make soap from scratch, the Department of Agricultural Services will provide you with information. You can then add rose petals and herbs to the cooling solution or use rose water in the actual cooking process. I'd love to see big slabs of pure castile in South Africa.

The secret with all soap making is to experiment. Hard water has a tremendous effect and it may be necessary to add more water if your water is hard. My experiments below were with soft borehole water that had run over quartz.

Rose petal soap
This is a very gentle soap that I dip into frequently when washing my hands. Its jellyness and setting ability will largely depend upon the soap you use. The harder the soap, the more water is needed to soften it. City tap water is often very hard, so you'll need to play around a bit to get the consistency you like. I set out basins on the lawn to catch rainwater – a practice that gives rise to many comments!

I never stop experimenting with this soap and often add chopped comfrey root (about 1 cup) to the rose petals. Comfrey root is mucilaginous, so I add an extra cup of the brew to my soap flakes. It sets into a soft, jelly-like consistency.

Boil 6 cups of water with 2 cups of rose petals. Simmer for 20 minutes, then cool, keeping well covered. In the meantime shred or grate a pure, mild soap until you have 2 cups. Strain the rose water, pour 3 cups of this fragrant liquid into a stainless steel pot and bring to the boil. Add the 2 cups of soap shavings and half a cup of

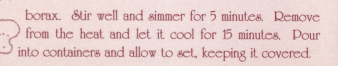

borax. Stir well and simmer for 5 minutes. Remove from the heat and let it cool for 15 minutes. Pour into containers and allow to set, keeping it covered.

Rose wash ball

A wash ball is a lovely way to soften the skin. Teenagers love using it for greasy skin on the back and shoulders.

Take a 30 cm square of thin cotton material like muslin or cheese cloth (no synthetics). Mix together 1 cup of oats, 1 cup of bran, 1 cup of rose petals and 1 cup of grated soap (choose a mild, neutral soap). Moisten with rose water to make it soft, then put in the centre of the cotton square and tie up the four corners, making a tight ball. Use this in the bath as a skin softening scrub for hard skin on the knees, elbows, heels and feet.

I hang my wash ball in the sun after my first bath and find it still works quite well for a second and even third bath. Ideally, however, one should use a fresh ball for every bath.

Cleansing rose soap

This is an exfoliator, so use it gently.

In the top of a double boiler place 2 cups of grated plain soap. Stir in 1 cup of homemade rose water until the soap has melted. Add 1 cup of finely chopped rose petals and finally 1 cup of mealie meal. Work it all together and keep adding a little warm water or more mealie meal until you get a thick consistency. When the mixture is cool enough to handle, grease your hands with a little oil and form the mixture into balls a little larger than a golf ball. Put the balls on greaseproof paper in an airy cupboard to dry, turning daily.

Rose soap bars
I make a batch or two of this twice a year — in spring and autumn when the roses are plentiful — to give away as presents. Simmer 2 cups of finely chopped red and pink rose petals in 1 cup of water in the top of a double boiler for 15 minutes. To vary, add half a cup of rosemary leaves, half a cup of chopped comfrey leaves or half a cup of violet flowers (*Viola odorata*), 10 cloves and a cinnamon stick. Remove from the heat, infuse until cool and strain.

Grate 1 cup of soap (I use white soap to get a pale pink end-product). Heat in the double boiler and add the strained rose and herb brew. Work it in well and add more soap flakes if necessary. You will need to experiment to get the consistency you like. For fragrance add a little rose essential oil. Pour the mixture into moulds that must be well oiled and lined with thin cotton material. (I use tiny bread tins measuring about 5 x 8 cm.) Leave to set, keeping the moulds covered with a cloth.

Before the bars harden completely pull off the material and rub off rough corners and marks with the back of a spoon. Leave to mature on greaseproof paper in a cupboard. Turn daily

until completely hard. Wrap in pretty paper and tie with a bow.

You can also make this soap with a thin cord or ribbon inserted to hang it from a tap. First tie the cord into a loop and then set the knot and part of the loop into the liquid soap to make sure it will not pull out.

Aloe, rose and comfrey jellied soap for dry, sensitive skins

Elderly people love this gentle, soothing soap. The best aloe to use here is *Aloe vera* – its soft jelly is superb – or, failing that, the jelly and juice of our indigenous bulbinella (*Bulbine frutescens*). Squeeze out the juice, slit the leaves and scrape off the jelly.

In a double boiler simmer 1 cup of finely minced comfrey leaves and root and 1 cup of finely chopped rose petals in 4 cups of water for 15 minutes. Take 1 cup of the hot liquid soap and briskly stir in 1 cup of aloe gel with a fork. Whisk at low speed until it is well blended (add a little water if necessary to keep it soft). Pour into a jar and use within a few days (the plant jelly does not keep).

Store the rest of the soap in a covered container in the fridge, taking out a cup at a time (you will need to reheat it and may have to add a little extra water to soften it). Add a fresh cup of aloe gel, thereby making up small batches as required.

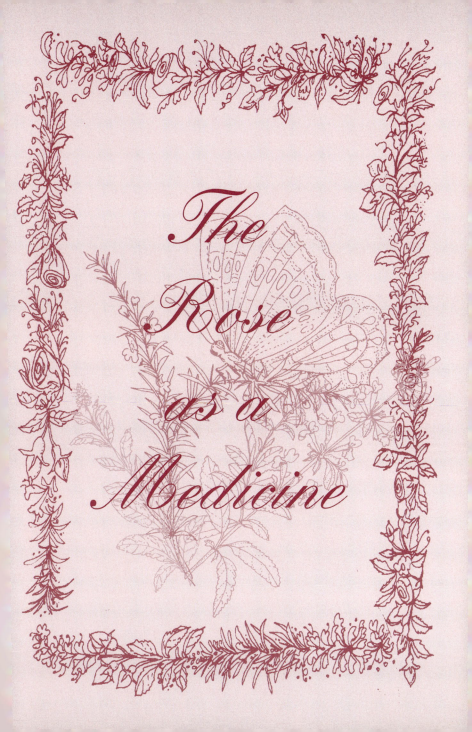

The Rose as a Medicine

*F*ew people ever consider the rose as a healing plant, but it has been used through the centuries to treat ailments from dropsy and ague to rheumatism, coughs and colds, and even epilepsy. To this day it forms the base for several medicines. Rosehips are well known for their high vitamin C content.

However, it is its ability to calm, quieten and relax for which the rose is known and which gives it a place in the world of natural medicine. In ancient herbals, the rose is often called the "woman's herb". I go along with this, since the rose is useful in treating premenstrual tension, hot flushes with heart palpitations, midlife crisis, tension, night sweat, anxiety, period pains, headache, insomnia and depression. It has been used successfully in treating hyperactivity and extreme tension, high blood pressure and irrational behaviour.

In former times, medicine was developed from two varieties, *Rosa gallica* and *R. centifolia*. The **British Pharmacopoeia** directs that only red rose petals from R. *gallica* be used and many hundreds of variations of these two ancient roses are in cultivation today. Interestingly, roses used in medicine must yield a deep red colour because the old herbalists considered the red rose to be more astringent and more binding than any of the other varieties. To quote one of these sages: "It strengtheneth the heart, the stomach, the liver and the retentive faculty, is good against all kinds of fluxes, prevents vomiting, stops tickling coughs, and is of service in consumption."

CAUTION: *The recipes in this book are in no way meant to replace your doctor. Always consult your doctor before starting a home treatment.*

Bladder conditions
Rosehips have been recorded as useful in treating bladder conditions. A decoction or syrup can be made for this purpose. (See recipes on page 44.)

Chills, colds and flu
I keep a bottle of rose brandy at the back of the cupboard for making a superb hot toddy. One tot in hot water cheers you up immediately. Even if you do not have a cold, it's a wonderful winter warmer!

Warm 2 cups of sugar, half a cup of finely sliced ripe rosehips, 1 cinnamon stock, 1 cup of rose petals, 12 cloves and 1 sprig of rosemary in 1 cup of brandy in the top of a double boiler. Simmer for 10 minutes, keeping covered. Add this mixture to a bottle of brandy, pushing in the rosemary sprig, the cinnamon stick and rose petals. Cork well and shake. Store in a dark cupboard and shake it up every now and then.

Take a tablespoon or two in a little hot water just before going to bed for colds and flu.

Anti-cold treatment
Rosehips have long been known to contain high levels of vitamin C, apart from tannin, pectin, carotene and a few fruit acids and oil. They are known to strengthen the body's

defences against infections and because of their remarkable components, make excellent tonics that relieve exhaustion, poor circulation and general debility, and combat colds.

Some hips are far better than others and rose growers will guide you as to which roses produce large, juicy hips. My favourite is the little pale pink dog rose, *Rosa canina*. It makes a huge, untidy, sprawling hedge and climber but its elongated bright red hips are abundant and beautiful.

Rosehip decoction
Gently simmer 3 teaspoons of chopped ripe rosehips (remove the stamen end and the stalk) in 1 cup of water for 10 minutes. Strain. Take 2 to 6 teaspoons daily at intervals, no more than 1 teaspoon at a time.

Rosehip syrup
Chop up 2 cups of ripe rosehips, stamen end and stalk removed. Add 2 cups of sugar, 1 1/2 cups of water and 1 cinnamon stick. Simmer for about 20 minutes in a covered pot or until the mixture becomes thick and syrupy. Strain through a sieve and bottle the syrup in a sterilised jar. It will keep indefinitely.

This syrup is an excellent cough remedy. Take a teaspoon whenever necessary, or stir 2 teaspoons of this syrup into half a cup of hot water.

Constipation
Rosehips have been recorded in helping cases of chronic constipation. A decoction or syrup can be made for this purpose (see recipes on page 44).

Corns
Mash 1 cup of rose petals into half a cup of apple cider vinegar. Add half a cup of minced comfrey root. Pound until well blended. Apply as a compress to corns or areas of hard skin. Keep covered for 25 minutes. Wash off with tepid water. Repeat each day for six days until the corn softens. A useful way to apply the mixture is to fill a sock with it and then wriggle the toes into it.

Depression
This is an ancient recipe for lifting the spirit and soothing an aching heart.

Pour 2 cups of boiling water over 2 cloves, half a cup of lemon balm and half a cup of red rose petals (Crimson Glory is loveliest here). Crush with a spoon to release the oils. Stand for 7 to 8 minutes, then strain. Sweeten with honey if desired. Have your tea with one vitamin B complex natural tablet, two dolomite tablets and a rose petal sandwich. You'll feel better immediately and your heavy heart will lift!

Eczema
Many soaps and hard water aggravate eczema

and dry skin. The rose has skin-softening properties and this compress will help soothe the irritation, particularly in the heat of midsummer.

Mix together 2 cups of finely pounded oats, 1 cup of roughly chopped rose petals and 1 cup of roughly chopped bulbinella leaves (*Bulbine frutescens*) with enough hot water to make a thick paste. Cover and allow to cool until pleasantly warm. It will swell and set after 10 minutes. Apply to the affected area, keeping it covered with a damp face cloth or towel so as to prevent the mixture drying out, and rest awhile. Wash off with tepid water and pat dry.

Gall bladder complaints
Rosehips have been recorded in helping mild gall bladder complaints. A decoction or syrup can be made for this purpose (see page 44).

Indigestion
I serve this tea at every dinner party. It will ease heartburn and indigestion.

To serve 4, pour 5 cups of boiling water over 1 cup of rose petals, half a cup to a cup of spearmint or peppermint, 10 cloves and 1 cinnamon stick. Allow to draw for 10 minutes. Strain, pour into small cups and sip slowly at the end of the meal. Float a fresh rose petal in each cup as you serve it. Everyone will love it!

Insomnia

This is the most pleasant of all nightcaps for those who can't sleep. Warm 1 cup of milk with a quarter of a cup of bruised rose petals and a quarter of a teaspoon of ground cloves for 5 minutes. Do not allow to boil. Strain, sweeten with a touch of honey if desired, add a dash of brandy if you have had a rough day and sip slowly after a warm bath. Rub rose cream (see page 26) into your feet. Sweet dreams!

Kidney conditions

Rosehips may be of benefit in mild kidney conditions. A decoction or syrup can be made for this purpose (see page 44).

Premenstrual tension and period pains

Pour 1 cup of boiling water over a quarter of a cup of bruised rose petals and a sprig of mint. Stand for 5 to 8 minutes, then strain. Sip while hot.

Stress and tension

Rose petal tea is considered to have a superb calming effect. I enjoy it as a nightcap with a leaf or two of rose-scented geranium (*Pelargonium graveolens*) in it.

Pour 1 cup of boiling water over a quarter of a cup of fresh red or pink rose petals and 3 rose-scented geranium leaves. Stand for 5 minutes. Strain and sweeten with a touch of honey if desired. Drink slowly.

Another excellent tea for tension headache is made by pouring 1 cup of boiling water over a quarter of a cup of bruised rose petals and a sprig of mint. Stand for 5 to 8 minutes, then strain. Sip while hot.

Rose petal tonic

This is my grandmother's recipe and will benefit all those who are overstressed and overstrained — excellent for exam-time anxieties.

½ cup rose petals
½ cup fresh peppermint
½ cup fresh rosemary
6 cloves
1 litre boiling water
juice of 1 lemon
2 tablespoons honey

Pour the boiling water over the petals, peppermint, rosemary and cloves. Allow to draw for 6 to 7 minutes. Strain, add lemon juice and honey. Drink a little at intervals throughout the day, either hot or cold. Keep in the fridge.

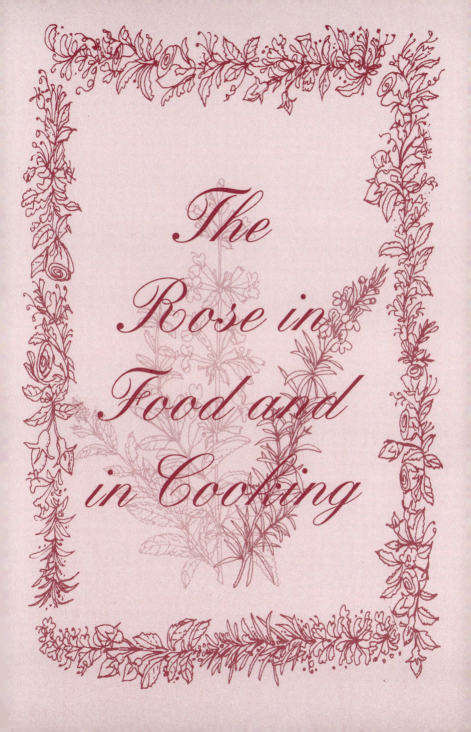

The Rose in Food and in Cooking

Not all roses are tasty, but some are tender, exquisite and taste just like a rose smells. One of the most delicious roses I have ever eaten is the new Margaret Roberts rose! It is tender and gentle and its abundance of pale pink petals which scatter the ground like a fairy carpet once the rose is full blown, are luscious and easily digested if caught before they fall. Experiment with your own roses and see which ones appeal to you most. Some have an almost musty taste, some are bitter and some are quite sweet.

The recipes throughout this book use unsprayed, unfertilised roses. Remember to remove the bitter white heel from the base of the rose petals.

Rose petal sandwiches

Picture a table spread for tea on a green lawn under a shady tree: a rose-patterned cloth on a white wicker table with rose-patterned cushions on white wicker chairs; tea cups with a rose design; a bowl of roses next to the rose-patterned tea pot; a plate of rose petal sandwiches decorated with roses and a great pink rose cake in the centre. A visual and fragrant feast – food for the gods!

Make rose petal sandwiches by slicing white bread very thinly and spread the slices with butter. Lay them close together, buttered side up. Dredge lightly with icing sugar, then spread thinly with cream cheese. Dust again with icing sugar, sprinkle a little chopped mint over the cream cheese and top with a thin layer of chopped, heeled pink and red rose petals. Cover each slice with a second slice spread with butter, cream cheese and dredged with icing sugar. Cut into triangles and serve on a bed of rose petals.

Rose petal salad
This will surely be the prettiest salad you have ever eaten!

1	butter lettuce torn into small pieces
1-2	cups chopped celery
1-2	cups chopped cucumber
1	cup thinly sliced fresh mushrooms
½	cup chopped fresh mint
2	cups diced green melon or spanspek
1	cup green sultana grapes
1-1½	cups multicolored rose petals, heeled

Mix together, decorate with extra rose petals and serve with a simple lemon dressing. It's refreshing, healthy and infinitely delicious and appealing! Serves 6 to 8.

Rose petal tea
To serve with rose petal sandwiches, this exquisite calming tea will help you unwind.

In a medium-sized teapot, place 1 sachet apple and cinnamon tea, black currant tea, or garden fruit tea, 6 leaves of rose-scented geranium, and half a cup of red rose petals. Fill with boiling water and allow to draw for at least 6 minutes. Sweeten with a touch of rose petal honey if desired. Serves 4.

Rose petal cake

This is an ordinary sponge or sandwich cake, with a few drops of rose essence instead of vanilla. It is the rose petal filling and icing that makes it so special.

Rose icing

±4 cups icing sugar
1   cup soft butter
     a little hot milk mixed with a little rose water (see page 23)
1   cup chopped pink rose petals

Mix the icing sugar into the butter, adding the warm milk and rose water a little at a time. When the icing is soft, well mixed and fairly stiff, add the rose petals and work in well. Spread between the two layers of the cake and on top of the cake. Use small movements to create a pattern in the icing. Decorate the cake all round with crystalised rose petals and also press some carefully on the top.

Crystallised rose petals

Choose a dry day and pick about 5 fully opened roses after the dew has evaporated. Dissolve 2 tablespoons of gum arabic in 2 cups of lukewarm water. Stir well. Separate the petals and dip each one into the gum arabic solution. Spread on trays lined with greaseproof paper and sprinkle with castor sugar. Leave to dry for 24 hours.

When I have not been able to find any gum arabic, I have used stiffly beaten egg white instead and on a dry, sunny day it too dries beautifully.

The next step is to make the petals crisp and crunchy. Make a syrup by boiling equal quantities of rose water (see page 23) and sugar for 30 minutes (thread stage). Using tweezers, carefully dip each petal into the syrup, place on oiled wire racks in a cool oven and leave the door ajar for 12 hours or longer until the petals are set and brittle. You can add cochineal to the syrup if you want a brighter pink colour.

Store the finished petals in an airtight container between layers of greaseproof paper.

ROSE PETAL HONEY
1   bottle clear, thin honey
1   cup heeled rose petals, lightly bruised

Gently heat the honey by standing the jar on a folded cloth in a saucepan of simmering water. Once it is warm to the touch push the rose petals into the jar one by one using a teaspoon. The petals need to have their entire surface covered, or they will rot. Remove from the heat and screw on the top. The honey will keep the petals beautifully preserved for months.

Spread on buttered toast or use as a cough mixture

with some lemon juice stirred in.

Rose petal conserve

This is an exquisite jam which I serve with hot scones, custards or rice puddings. It is so popular that I never seem to have enough!

450 g	white sugar
	juice of 4 lemons
1	cinnamon stick
1,2	litres water
225 g	red and pink rose petals, heeled

Boil the sugar, lemon juice, cinnamon stick and water together, stirring carefully with a wooden spoon until all the sugar is dissolved. Add the heeled rose petals. Simmer gently and scoop off the froth that rises. Simmer until the jam thickens, usually between 30 and 40 minutes. Pour into small hot jars. Seal each jar with a layer of melted wax. Screw on the lids while hot and store labelled in a cool cupboard.

Rose ice cream

This is a knock-out served at Christmas with Christmas pudding.

1	tin condensed milk
	juice of 3 lemons
1	cup rose petals, heeled and sprinkled with 1 cup of castor sugar
500 ml	thick cream, well whisked

Whisk the lemon juice into the condensed milk — it will start to thicken immediately. Add the heeled rose petal and castor sugar mixture, whisk well, then fold in the stiffly whisked cream. Pour into freezing trays and freeze. Serve sprinkled with rose petals or crystalised rose petals (see page 52). Serves 6 to 8.

Rose petal curd

Made like lemon curd but containing rose petals, this is a gourmet's delight. Serve it on pancakes or hot scones, on rice pudding or in éclairs, or best of all, on top of sliced bananas with whipped cream and a sprinkling of mint and almonds. I always keep some of this curd in the fridge to whip up a quick pudding for unexpected guests. It also makes a superb gift.

1	cup butter, roughly diced
3	eggs, well beaten
1	cup white sugar
	juice of 3 lemons
1	cup finely chopped rose petals
2	teaspoons finely grated lemon rind

Melt the butter in the top of a double boiler. Meanwhile whisk the eggs and the sugar until creamy. Add the lemon juice and rind to the butter. Gradually add the whisked eggs and sugar, stirring all the time. Add the rose petals and stir until it thickens. Pour into hot jars, cover with a piece of greaseproof paper that has been dipped in brandy and screw on the lid. Leave to cool. Store

in the fridge and use within 2 months.

Scented Rose Cream

This is a lovely way of flavouring cream to serve with fruit salads and desserts. I also find it superb as an "icing" for a chocolate cake or for filling chocolate éclairs.

The day before you will need the cream, pick 2 or 3 cups of fragrant rose petals and lay them in a flat dish. Sprinkle with castor sugar to cover. Top with another layer of petals, cover with plastic cling wrap and leave overnight.

Next morning shake out the petals, discard them and sieve the castor sugar. Whip 2 cups of thick cream until stiff, add half a cup to a cup of the rose-flavoured and scented castor sugar (depending on how sweet you like it) and fold in approximately half a cup of finely chopped rose petals. (Remember to remove the bitter white heel from each rose petal before chopping them.) For more colour add more petals. For a confetti effect, I use richly scented roses of all colours.

I serve this cream with fruit salad in small glass bowls decorated all round the rim with multi-coloured rose petals. It looks stunning!

Rose Wine
For a special occasion this takes some beating.
1   bottle rosé wine
3   tablespoons rose petal syrup (see page 57)
1   cup rose petals

Camphor basil

Pour out a little wine from the bottle, add the rose petals and the syrup. Cork and shake well. Leave to steep for 2 hours, then chill. The wine is now ready for serving. Float a rose petal in each glass.

Rose petal syrup
1	cup red rose petals
1	cup water
1	cup sugar

Boil the rose petals in the water and sugar for 15 minutes. Strain.

Rose punch
I often serve this at a party and have found all age groups love it: it is refreshing, thirst quenching and contains no alcohol. Should you want to, you may add 1 bottle of rosé wine after the punch has been chilled.

1	litre boiling water
1	cup lemon verbena leaves (or lemon balm (melissa) or lemon grass), chopped
2	cups red rose petals
2	cups rose petal syrup (see recipe above)
2	litres unsweetened, unpreserved fruit juice (litchi or orange and mango juice is delicious) lemon slices, rose petals and mint leaves to decorate

Pour the boiling water over the leaves and rose petals.

Stand until cool, then strain. Add the rose petal syrup and fruit juice and stir well. Chill. Pour into a punch bowl or pretty glasses. Float lemon slices, rose petals and mint leaves on top. Serves 10 to 12.

ROSE LIQUEUR

This easy-to-make liqueur is a tantalising end to a festive dinner and also makes a lovely gift. Dribble a little over ice cream or fruit salad, or add a dash to punches and cool drinks.

750 ml	vodka or cane spirit
2	cups rose petals
1	cup white sugar
1	cup water

Remove the bitter white heel from the base of the rose petals and lightly bruise them. Pack into a bottle.

Warm the vodka gently, pour over the petals and cork. Leave corked for 2 to 3 weeks, giving it a daily shake. Strain, dissolve the sugar in the water and boil for 10 minutes with 1 cup of heeled red rose petals. Allow to cool, then strain and add to the vodka and rose petal mixture.

Pour into a pretty bottle and serve in tiny liqueur glasses. Sip slowly to truly savour the rose petal fragrance.

Several centuries ago, fragrant flowers and leaves were far more important than they are today as they were used to disguise the unpleasant odours brought about by open sewers, poor hygiene and a lack of running water. Gardens and fields of fragrant flowers were cultivated for this purpose and in each house, even simple cottages, a small room — called a "still room" — was set aside, often under the stairs, for the lady of the house to make her fragrant oils and lotions, pomanders, pot-pourris, tussie mussies and "sweet balls".

Through the years, with progress in standards of hygiene and plumbing, the art of creating these fragrant delights was gradually lost. Yet we still have those age-old recipes to link us with the past, and in many of them the rose features prominently.

Rose Tussie Mussie
One of the easiest ways of preserving the beauty and fragrance of roses is to tie buds that are just showing colour into a tight posy, or tussie mussie. Ring with lavender and rosemary or myrtle sprigs, push a cinnamon stick well down into the centre and tie with ribbon. Its prettiness will be preserved when it dries. Fragrant rose essential oil (bought from your chemist) can be dripped into its heart so the cinnamon stick — which acts as a fixative — can absorb it.

Hang or stand your posy in a cupboard to keep it well scented, reviving it from time to time with a few drops of rose oil. You will enjoy each posy for years to come.

Rose Pot-Pourri
Below are two recipes for basic rose pot-pourri, using the wet or

the dry methods. You can experiment with additional ingredients until you find a mixture you like.

Dry rose pot-pourri
On a dry day collect a basket of roses. Pull the petals off the calyx and sprinkle them on newspaper-lined trays or on wire mesh trays and store in the shade. Turn daily until dry.

Mix together 3 cups of minced, dried lemon peel, 1 cup of roughly broken cinnamon pieces, 1 cup of whole cloves, 1 cup of coriander seeds and a few drops of rose essential oil. Store in a sealed jar for 10 to 14 days, giving it a daily shake. Add more rose oil from time to time – the secret here is to really saturate the spices with as much fragrance as you can afford.

After 10 to 14 days, mix the now heady spice into 10 to 15 cups of dried rose petals, and add more oil if desired. Store in a sealed container for another 10 to 14 days, again giving it a daily shake. It has to smell rich and strong. Put in bowls or sachets and revive from time to time with a little rose essential oil.

Wet rose pot-pourri
This is a most exciting way of making a deeply fragrant, soul-stirring, old-fashioned "rotten pot", which is the old meaning of the French word "pot pourri' – a mixture of rotting leaves and flowers! But far from rotten it is, for it smells remarkable even in its early preparation stages. Wet pot-pourri doesn't look as pretty as dry

 potpourri, but it does smell wonderful and lasts exceptionally well.

Find a large crock or jar that has a wide mouth and a tight-fitting lid. Pick some roses and separate the petals, discarding the calyx. Place a layer of petals into the crock, cover with a layer of coarse sea salt and a thin layer of roughly ground cloves, cinnamon, nutmeg and coriander. (I combine a cup of each and keep it well mixed by giving it a daily shake in a closed jar which I keep at hand for whenever I have any fresh petals to add to the crock.)

Cover with more rose petals (and fresh lavender flowers, rose-scented geranium leaves, narcissus flowers, sweet peas, etc. if desired) and then add more salt and spices. Every time you add a layer be sure to seal it well, for the air should not reach the contents.

As the wet petals mature, you'll find a rather strange, mildew-like scum rising. Stir the contents, add more oil and continue. You'll need to break up the "cakes" of petals and spices. I do this until my crock is full. I leave it to finally mature for a month, by which time it is simply incredible – dark, strong and seductive! Break it up again and mix well. Pack it into small jars – I love the ones with holes in their lids – and place all about the house. It will last for years and only needs the occasional revival of a few drops of rose oil to maintain its rich fragrance.

Rose petal spice jar
I love this spice jar in a bathroom or toilet, or as a Christmas gift.

You can also put the spices into lace-edged muslin or voile circles tied with pretty ribbons to hang behind the bathroom door or in a cupboard. I find it very useful in keeping cupboards at the sea smelling fresh. An added bonus: moths and fishmoths cannot stand it!

Mix minced, dried lemon peel and cloves with rose essential oil and clove oil. Store in a closed jar for several days to let the oil penetrate the spices. Give it a daily shake.

Into each jar pack layer upon layer of dried rose petals, roughly broken cinnamon sticks, coriander seeds, minced dried orange peel, small dried fir cones, dried rosehips, dried myrtle berries, dried bay leaves, dried cypress leaves, twigs and bark, dried rosemary sprigs and the dried lemon peel and clove mixture. Tuck a small lemon spiked with cloves in the centre, covering it up with all the other ingredients. Add a few more drops of oil and seal for 10 to 14 days. This will help saturation and blending. Remove the lid and let the spicy fragrance drift everywhere.

Rosebud ball

For a really exquisite gift, nothing touches this beautiful fragrant ball. You will need at least 60 to 80 dried rosebuds on 6 cm stems. Multicoloured roses look lovely.

Cut two bowl-shaped pieces out of two large blocks of oasis so that fitted together they make a ball. Hollow out a tennis ball-sized space from inside both pieces — don't be too fussy about getting the

spheres perfectly round. The outer covering of the rosebuds will cover any irregularities.

Mix together 1 cup of crushed coriander seeds, crushed cloves, crushed nutmeg and broken cinnamon pieces, rose essential oil and 1 cup of semi-dry rose petals. Pound together to make a paste with rose essential oil and some homemade rose water.

Fill one half of the oasis with the spice rose mixture, which will be fairly sticky, and heap it up. Cover with the other half and piece together with wire. Then press in the rosebuds close together to cover the whole ball. Pierce a few holes into the ball with a knitting needle to enable the spice perfume to escape.

Leave a hole the size of a pencil on top so that you can drip a little oil into the core from time to time. Suspend by means of a pretty ribbon tied onto a wire loop which you press into the ball.

Rose peace pillow

This lovely neck support is a boon to those who are tense and restless and is especially helpful for the traveller.

For a pillow measuring 40 x 26 cm, make a sachet of 16 x 16 cm. Mix together 1 cup of dried rose petals and 1 cup of minced dried lemon peel soaked in 4 teaspoons of rose essential oil. Add half a cup of cinnamon pieces and half a cup of cloves. Add more rose oil and mix well with the lemon peel. Add the rose petals and stand for 10 days in a screwtop jar, giving it a daily shake. Stuff into the small sachet.

Yarrow

Make a lining for the pillow and fill with foam chips. Nestle the fragrant sachet in the middle and sew up. Make a pretty rose design cover and edge it with lace. Every few months, unpick the lining and the inner sachet, shake out the contents, add more rose oil and shake it up in a bottle for 3 or 4 days before refilling the sachet. Wash the lining and cover before returning the chips with the freshly fragrant sachet. Your pillow will be brand new!

Rose-scented paper
This is the old-fashioned way of using pot-pourri to scent writing paper, wrapping paper and drawer lining paper. I love it so much I use it to scent cards and envelopes, gift tags and even little notebooks.

Take an airtight container as large as you can find. (I use a huge bin.) Drip about 2 tablespoons of rose essential oil over half a bucket of thinly pared, dried lemon peel and keep in a sealed jar for 10 days. Give it a daily shake. Add to this 1 bucket of dried rose petals. In the large bin, put a deep layer of petals and peel. Cover with a sheet of blotting paper, to prevent the oil from coming into contact with the writing paper.

Loosely place your writing paper, note paper, etc. on top of the blotting paper so that the scent can penetrate it, and cover with another layer of blotting paper. Sprinkle with more peel and petals, layer more blotting paper, more writing paper, etc. Repeat until your bin is full. Seal.

The lemon peel "fixes" the oil. You can also add cloves, crushed nutmeg, cinnamon pieces and coriander seeds to make the mixture more spicy.

I keep my writing paper in my bin, adding more rose petals peel soaked in essential oil from time to time.

ROSE BEADS

Church rosaries were once made of rose petals, hence the name. The beads were polished by the continuous movement of fingers on them and at the same time emitted a delicate rose fragrance. I have experimented through the years and have found, much to my delight, that the ones I made with my little four-year-old daughter 20 years ago are still sweetly fragrant!

Mince about 10 cups of fresh rose petals so that you end up with 4 cups of moist pulp. Heat – do not boil – for 10 minutes with 2 cups of water. Cool. Add 2 teaspoons of essential oil, 2 tablespoons of ground cinnamon, 1 tablespoon of ground cloves and 2 tablespoons of finely crushed gum benzoin.

Mix everything together in a pestle and mortar and add extra rose water to make a paste. If the mixture does not bind quickly, work in 1 to 3 tablespoons of cake flour mixed with a little water. Rub your hands with oil and, pinching off little bits of the rose pulp, roll it into marble-sized balls. Place the balls on greaseproof paper. Before the beads are dry, pierce with an oiled darning needle and thread with thin, strong cotton or nylon fishing line, leaving spaces in between.

It will take three or four days for the beads to dry completely. Move the beads on the line frequently to keep them loose. Tucked among your clothes, you can savour the magic of their old-fashioned fragrance.

Rose pastilles

These rather unusual rose-scented shapes were once used as incense in holy places, to keep clothes and blankets mothproof, and to scent linen kists in which trousseaus were stored. Some that have been found to come from the fifteenth century are still faintly fragrant. I tuck them among books, behind my files and in my sewing basket, as well as among jerseys and winter woollies.

Gently simmer 8 cups of rose petals in 3 cups of water for 15 minutes. Allow to cool. Add 1 cup of ground gum benzoin, 1 cup of ground mixed cinnamon and cloves and 1 cup of crushed coriander seeds. Add rose essential oil and mix well to form a paste. Add a little more gum benzoin if the mixture is too moist.

Line ice trays with plastic film, grease with a little cooking oil and pack each cube with the pulp. Cover and let it harden and dry. If the pulp holds its shape it can be pressed into rounds or ovals and placed on oiled greaseproof paper to harden.

Once dry, rub with a touch of rose oil. Tuck the pastilles behind the seats or in the door pockets of your car or put them in a musty cup-

board. For added fragrance, rub on a little rose oil from time to time.

Rose-scented candles

Line candle moulds, tins or yoghurt containers with foil or cling wrap. Fix pieces of string for wicks into the moulds by pushing the wicks through a hole in the bottom and tying a knot. Tie them to a pencil at the top which rests on the rim. Secure the bottom knot with plasticine so that the hot wax does not seep through.

Melt 500 g paraffin wax or plain white candles. Add a piece of red wax crayon, shaved, to give it a pretty pink colour. When the mixture has cooled somewhat, but still remains liquid, add 1 cup of dried rose petals with a little rose essential oil and stir gently until well distributed. Add more rose oil if desired.

Pour the wax into the moulds. Carefully position pressed maidenhair fern and rose petals down the sides of the moulds with the handle of a spoon. Allow to cool.

When set, shake out, or tear off the sides of the containers. Top up around the wick with a little more melted wax and paint over rough patches, decorating with more ferns and petals if needed. Fix the decorations by painting over with warm wax.

Mature for 4 to 5 days, then polish the candles with a pad of cotton wool dipped in a little sunflower oil or your own rose oil. Add a few drops of rose essential oil for extra fragrance.

Epilogue

𝒜nd so we come to the end of our walk through my garden of roses. My hope is that you are inspired and uplifted and eagerly planning your own garden of fragrance and beauty. May it be a source of constant delight, interest and joy.

I once heard an unforgettable comment from a most wonderful man who was well into his nineties: "You'll find gardeners do not grow old the way their peers do. You see, they have something to look forward to every day throughout every season, and when mid-winter is upon us, there will be the memories of summer and the anticipation of spring. There isn't time to grow old!" What a thought!

On a visit to the beautiful Gardens of the Rose in England a few years ago, the elderly guide told us of the gardens of remembrance that some rose growers were creating in communities, in little villages, in city waste areas and in their own gardens as a tribute to special friends or to loved ones who had passed on. These places of peace and beauty — sometimes large and breathtaking, sometimes small and intimate — were planted with roses in loving memory of someone special, whose name was inscribed on a little plaque nestled at the rose's roots. These living memories will bloom year after year, providing a place where all can come and rest awhile on the benches and stone walls, to smell the roses, enjoy their beauty and to take with them some measure of peace into the busy world.

I shall plant roses for friends and loved ones too. I shall make a garden of memories and what joy there will be in this collection!

My last words to you, rose lover, are taken from a wonderful old Irish blessing:

Sure, and may there be a path of smoothness before you, and it bordered with roses such have never been seen nor smelt before for the warm, fine colour and the great beauty and the deep perfume that is in them.

And I wish to add: may there be joy every inch of the way.

> Margaret Roberts
> Herbal Centre
> De Wildt
> Transvaal
> South Africa

INDEX

Ageing skin	33
Anti-cold treatment	43
Ants	12, 13, 14
Aphids	8, 12, 13, 14, 15, 17
Attar of roses	28
Bath milk	25
Bath vinegar	31
Beads, rose	66
Beauty treatments	21-40
Beetles, rose	14, 15, 16, 19-20
Black spot	10
Bladder conditions	43
Cake, rose petal	52
Camphor basil	7
Catmint	8
Chills	43
Colds	43
Comfrey	6
Conserve, rose petal	54
Constipation	45
Cooking with roses	49-58
Corns	45
Cosmetics	21-40
Cotton lavender	8
Cream, scented rose	56
Creeping rosemary	14
Crickets	15
Crystallised petals	52
Curd, rose petal	55
Cutworms	17
Depression	45
Dry pot-pourri	61
Eczema	45
Emollient cream	26
Face packs	32-6
Fertilizers, natural	5-7
Flu	43
Foliar feed	9
Food, roses in	49-58
Freshener	24
Gall bladder complaints	46
Growing roses	3-20
Hair vinegar	31
Herbs, insect-repelling	7
Honey, rose petal	53
Horsetail	9
Ice cream, rose petal	54
Iceberg rose	4
Icing, rose petal	52
Indigestion	46
Insect repellents	7-8, 12, 14, 18
Insomnia	47
Jellied soap	40
Khakibos	10
Kidney conditions	47
Lemon thyme	10
Liqueur	58
Lucerne	6
Margaret Roberts rose	2
Marigold	11
Massage oil	28
Mealie bugs	12, 13
Medicine, rose as	41-8
Mildew	8, 9, 10, 18
Moisturisers	25, 26
Moles	11, 12
Myrtle	11, 12
Natural fertilizers	5-7
Nematodes	11
Nettle, stinging	6
Oil, rose	27, 29
Pastilles, rose	67
Paul Scarlet rose	4
Peace pillow	64
Pennyroyal	12
Period pains	47
Planting roses	4-5
Pot-pourri	59-68
Premenstrual tension	47
Punch	57
Pyrethrum	12
Queen Elizabeth rose	4
Red spider	8, 13
Rose oil	27
Rose beetles	14, 15, 16, 19-20
Rose water	23
Rosebud ball	63
Rosehip decoction	44
Rosehip syrup	44
Rosemary	13
Rue	14
Sage	6
Salad, rose petal	51
Sandwiches, rose petal	50
Scale	8, 13
Scented candles	68
Scented paper	65
Scented rose cream	56
Soap	36-40
Southernwood	15
Spice jar	62
Stinging nettle	6
Stress	47
Syrup	
rose petal	57
rosehip	44
Talisman rose	4
Tansy	15
Tea, rose petal	51
Thyme, lemon	10
Tussie mussie	60
Vinegar	30-2
Wash ball, rose	38
Wet pot-pourri	61
Wild ginger	16
Wilde als	16
Wine, rose	56
Winter savory	17
Wormwood	17
Yarrow	18